John Jay

*First Chief Justice of
the Supreme Court*

Colonial Leaders

Lord Baltimore
English Politician and Colonist

Benjamin Banneker
American Mathematician and Astronomer

Sir William Berkeley
Governor of Virginia

William Bradford
Governor of Plymouth Colony

Jonathan Edwards
Colonial Religious Leader

Benjamin Franklin
American Statesman, Scientist, and Writer

Anne Hutchinson
Religious Leader

Cotton Mather
Author, Clergyman, and Scholar

Increase Mather
Clergyman and Scholar

James Oglethorpe
Humanitarian and Soldier

William Penn
Founder of Democracy

Sir Walter Raleigh
English Explorer and Author

Caesar Rodney
American Patriot

John Smith
English Explorer and Colonist

Miles Standish
Plymouth Colony Leader

Peter Stuyvesant
Dutch Military Leader

George Whitefield
Clergyman and Scholar

Roger Williams
Founder of Rhode Island

John Winthrop
Politician and Statesman

John Peter Zenger
Free Press Advocate

Revolutionary War Leaders

John Adams
Second U.S. President

Ethan Allen
Revolutionary Hero

Benedict Arnold
Traitor to the Cause

King George III
English Monarch

Nathanael Greene
Military Leader

Nathan Hale
Revolutionary Hero

Alexander Hamilton
First U.S. Secretary of the Treasury

John Hancock
President of the Continental Congress

Patrick Henry
American Statesman and Speaker

John Jay
First Chief Justice of the Supreme Court

Thomas Jefferson
Author of the Declaration of Independence

John Paul Jones
Father of the U.S. Navy

Lafayette
French Freedom Fighter

James Madison
Father of the Constitution

Francis Marion
The Swamp Fox

James Monroe
American Statesman

Thomas Paine
Political Writer

Paul Revere
American Patriot

Betsy Ross
American Patriot

George Washington
First U.S. President

Famous Figures of the Civil War Era

Jefferson Davis
Confederate President

Frederick Douglass
Abolitionist and Author

Ulysses S. Grant
Military Leader and President

Stonewall Jackson
Confederate General

Robert E. Lee
Confederate General

Abraham Lincoln
Civil War President

William Sherman
Union General

Harriet Beecher Stowe
Author of Uncle Tom's Cabin

Sojourner Truth
Abolitionist, Suffragist, and Preacher

Harriet Tubman
Leader of the Underground Railroad

John Jay

First Chief Justice of the Supreme Court

Phelan Powell

Arthur M. Schlesinger, jr.
Senior Consulting Editor

Chelsea House Publishers

Philadelphia

Produced by 21st Century Publishing and Communications, Inc.
New York, NY. http://www.21cpc.com

CHELSEA HOUSE PUBLISHERS
Production Manager Pamela Loos
Art Director Sara Davis
Director of Photography Judy L. Hasday
Managing Editor James D. Gallagher
Senior Production Editor J. Christopher Higgins

Staff for *JOHN JAY*
Project Editor/Publishing Coordinator Jim McAvoy
Project Editor Anne Hill
Associate Art Director Takeshi Takahashi
Series Design Keith Trego

The Chelsea House World Wide Web address is
http://www.chelseahouse.com

First Printing
1 3 5 7 9 8 6 4 2

Library of Congress Cataloging-in-Publication Data

Powell, Phelan.
    John Jay / Phelan Powell.
        p.   cm. — (Revolutionary War leaders)
    Includes bibliographical references and index.
    ISBN 0-7910-5979-0 (hc) — 0-7910-6137-X (pbk.)
    1. Jay, John, 1745-1829—Juvenile literature. 2. Statesmen—United
    States—Biography—Juvenile literature. 3. United States—
    Politics and government—1775-1783—Juvenile literature. 4. United
    States—Politics and government—1783-1809—Juvenile literature.
    5. Judges—New York (State)—Biography—Juvenile literature. 6. New
    York (State)—Politics and government—To 1775—Juvenile literature.
    [1. Jay, John, 1745-1829. 2. Statesmen.] I. Title. II. Series.

    E302.6.J4 P68 2000
    973.3'092—dc21
    [B]   00-038377
                                                                      CIP

Publisher's Note: In Colonial and Revolutionary War America, there were no standard rules for spelling, punctuation, capitalization, or grammar. Some of the quotations that appear in the Colonial Leaders and Revolutionary War Leaders series come from original documents and letters written during this time in history. Original quotations reflect writing inconsistencies of the period.

Contents

New York was one of the largest and most important of the 13 American colonies. John was born in New York City. He also attended college and later set up a law practice there.

Strong Beginnings

When John Jay was born in New York City on December 12, 1745, there was no New York State and no United States as we know them today. New York was a **colony** ruled by Great Britain, which is far across the Atlantic Ocean. Great Britain also ruled the 12 other colonies that later became states. No one knew at the time of John's birth that he was destined to be the first man ever to refer to the 13 colonies as the United States.

John's ancestors came from France, where his great-grandfather, Pierre Jay, had been a business-man. Pierre Jay was a **Huguenot**. At that time in

John's father was a respected member of New York society who prospered with his import-export business.

France, Huguenots suffered **persecution** because of their religious beliefs. Pierre Jay fled to England, where his son, Augustus, grew up. When Augustus became an adult, he sailed to the colony of New York, where he married Anna

Maria Bayard. Taking advantage of the thriving colonial economy, Augustus started a successful import-export business.

Augustus's son, Peter, learned the business from his father and eventually became his father's partner. By the time Peter married Mary Van Cortlandt, daughter of a prominent Dutch family, he was a wealthy and well-respected member of New York society. Peter and Mary's family eventually included eight children. John was the sixth son and the youngest child. By the time John was born, 40-year-old Peter had done so well as a businessman that he was able to retire. So the family moved to a farmhouse in the village of Rye, New York.

While his father's life became more relaxed, John's education was just beginning. He learned Latin and English from his mother and developed a love of reading at an early age. John's father realized, even when the boy was only seven, that he was very special. Young John showed great promise as a scholar.

As was often the practice at the time, formal schooling was taught in a church, and sometimes children had to leave home to attend school. At the age of 11, John left his parents for the school at the French Huguenot Church in the town of New Rochelle. The boy lived in the home of the pastor, Peter Stoope, who conducted classes and all conversation in French, the native language of John's Huguenot ancestors.

In colonial times, a young man who showed scholarly ability could go on to college at a very young age. When he was 14, John entered King's College (now Columbia University) in New York City. His record at the college was spotless except for an incident that took place just before he graduated in 1764. Some of John's friends had caused some damage at the college, and he knew who they were. Not wanting to get his friends in trouble, John wouldn't tell officials who was responsible. He was punished by being forced to leave college for a time. But officials were so impressed with the young man's ability to speak

John proved to be an excellent student when he attended King's College in New York City. Although still in his teens, he was a fine speaker who was able to express his ideas clearly and reasonably.

clearly and make his case that they allowed him to attend graduation. He was also given the opportunity to speak at the ceremonies on the subject of peace. At the time, John could not imagine that he would spend much of his life aiding his fellow citizens in their search for peace.

In the 1760s and 1770s, the subject of peace was very much on the minds of the American colonists. When John was still a boy, Great Britain and France had begun a war to decide who would rule the lands in North America. The French, who had settled what is now Canada, began moving south into the Ohio Valley in the mid-1750s. They set up forts and trading posts in territory claimed by Britain. In 1754, the British decided to drive the French back into Canada, and the French and Indian War began. It was called that because most Native Americans sided with the French.

For nine years, Britain and France fought for control of North America. Because the British had more soldiers and supplies, they finally drove the French from Ohio and went on to invade Canada. When British soldiers captured the city of Montreal, the French surrendered and signed a peace **treaty**. By the time John was in college, Britain controlled all of Ohio and ruled Canada.

But problems still remained. Many American settlers were moving west into the Ohio Valley to farm and set up towns. As they settled, they pushed Native Americans off the land, and the Indians fought back. Determined to drive off settlers, Native American tribes attacked farms and towns all along the western **frontier** and destroyed many British forts and trading posts. After several battles, British soldiers and American settlers finally crushed the Indian uprising. It now seemed that people could safely move westward.

But the British government had other ideas. Britain wanted the friendship of the Indians to protect its fur trade. The government also did not want to pay the costs of stationing British soldiers along the frontier to protect settlers. Much to the resentment of colonists, the English king, George III, made a **proclamation** forbidding settlers from moving beyond the Appalachian Mountains. The king ruled that all the land west of the mountains belonged to Native Americans.

Many colonists were enraged by the king's

As colonists pushed west, they settled on land belonging to American Indians. In 1763, under the leadership of a great chief, Pontiac, 40 Indian tribes rose up in rebellion. In only a few weeks, Pontiac and his brave warriors destroyed nearly every British fort and settlement along the frontier. But Pontiac could not gain the support of several important tribes. When British soldiers and settlers struck back and won several battles, Pontiac's rebellion failed.

proclamation. They had fought on the side of the British and sent many men and supplies to help defeat the French. The colonists resented the fact that the king had not consulted them about the lands in the West. And they felt that Britain was taking territory they had fought hard to win for themselves.

Many colonists also quarreled with the British over other rules and regulations. The French and Indian War had been costly for Britain. In order to pay for the war, the government put heavier taxes on many goods the colonists bought and sold. In addition, Britain restricted the colonists' trade with other nations, so merchants could not make much profit. To save money, Britain also required

Most Native Americans sided with the French against the British and the colonists in the French and Indian War. Here, American settlers along the frontier repel an Indian attack during the war.

colonists to pay for the upkeep of British soldiers. Colonists were especially resentful of the rules because they did not have a voice in these decisions. The British government simply passed the laws and expected the colonists to obey them without question.

Resentment and anger against Britain was

building up when John set up his law practice in New York City in 1768. Although he was living in a time of growing conflict between Britain and the colonies, John did not become involved in the protests. With his law partner, Robert Livingston, he was becoming a successful attorney. Although an honorable pursuit, law was not an easy path for a young man to follow. There were no typewriters or computers to gather information or write out documents. Everything was handwritten, which proved a very time-consuming process.

Being a lawyer at that time was also not terribly exciting. Much of John's work involved collecting debts for his clients. But he was successful and earned a reputation as a hard worker and a young man with strong reasoning powers. John also enjoyed a happy and quiet personal life. He often met with friends for evenings of pleasant companionship and discussions of points of law. When he was 26, John wrote a friend, telling him how fortunate he felt about his life thus far. "With respect to business, I am as well circumstanced as I have a right to expect; my old friends contribute much to my happiness, and upon the whole I have reason to be satisfied with my share of the attention of Providence."

John, it seemed, would remain a quiet, serious, and successful young lawyer in a private practice. But in 1773, he took a step that would lead him into a lifelong career in public service. The New Jersey and New York colonies were involved in a boundary dispute. John was chosen as a member of a royal commission to help settle the conflict. His work on the commission gained him the attention of leaders who would later call upon him to serve his country in troubled times.

John did not begin public life alone. In 1774, he married Sarah Livingston. Sarah, whose father, William Livingston, would soon become governor of New Jersey, was known for her beauty and social graces. Their union began in a loving relationship which lasted a lifetime. Together, John and Sarah entered what was to be the most revolutionary time in our nation's history.

American colonists worked hard to farm, trade, and build towns and cities. They also believed in making many of their own rules to govern themselves. When Great Britain tried to gain more control over the colonists, they grew angry and resentful.

A Restless America

From the time the 13 American colonies were founded, people from England and Europe had crossed the ocean to seek their fortunes in a new world. From Georgia in the south to New Hampshire in the north, colonists farmed, traded, and built towns and cities to make new lives for themselves. Many hearty settlers crossed the Appalachian Mountains, moving west toward the mighty Mississippi River.

Even though colonists were ruled by Great Britain, they had set up many of their own rules and laws to govern themselves. They strongly believed in **representative government** and in electing their own local leaders. Because Britain was so far away, colonists had learned to depend on thcmselves. They were beginning to develop democratic ideas. Then the British government insisted on more taxes and began interfering with the colonists' freedom to import and export goods. This angered many colonists, and the stage was set for conflict with the British.

As early as 1763, leaders like Patrick Henry of Virginia were protesting the new taxes. It was, they said, "taxation without representation" because colonists had no voice in the British government. By 1770, colonists, many of them fiery and hot tempered, were openly protesting in the streets of the cities and through newspapers and pamphlets. The more they protested, the more taxes Britain imposed— and the more soldiers the government sent to collect the taxes.

John did not raise his voice in protest or express ideas of separating from Britain. Even though he was of French ancestry, he considered

Patrick Henry gives an impassioned speech to the Virginia legislature. His powerful words moved many Americans to protest taxation without representation.

himself a loyal subject of King George III. As a friend of the colonial leader Benjamin Franklin, John often shared ideas with the older man. Like

John, Franklin at first believed that the colonies should remain part of Great Britain, but with more freedoms. With such an arrangement, Franklin reasoned, a revolution leading to separation might be avoided.

In those days, communication among the colonies was poor. There were few good roads, and travel by horseback, wagon, or stagecoach was difficult and slow. Colonists in South Carolina would not always know what was going on in Massachusetts. Colonial leaders decided to set up committees in each colony to discuss current events and keep in touch with one another. In New York City, John became a member of the Committee of Fifty-One. Its members held meetings at a local coffee house and wrote statements of American rights and complaints which were sent to other colonies. These committees were important in helping unite colonists and strengthen their opposition to British policies.

Spreading the messages from colony to colony was often dangerous. Messengers, such as the famous Paul Revere of Boston, would speed off on their horses to take the news to nearby colonies. Then, other messengers would carry the news farther. Messengers had to dash past red-coated British soldiers along the way. People often had to read the messages by candlelight behind locked and bolted doors.

While messages were going back and forth among the colonies, an event occurred that stirred the colonists to great anger. In 1773, Britain put a heavy tax on tea, the colonists' favorite drink, which was carried to America on British ships. Furious colonists declared they would defy the law when any tea ships arrived at their port cities. In Philadelphia and New York, crowds of colonists turned back the tea ships. But in Boston, the ships' captains refused to leave. Then, on a cold night in December 1773, a group of men dressed up as Native Americans boarded the Boston tea ships and dumped all the tea into the dark waters of the harbor.

The Boston Tea Party, as it came to be known,

John was a member of a New York committee, like this one, which met to discuss news about events throughout the colonies.

infuriated British officials, and they decided to teach the colonists a lesson. Officials closed Boston's port to trade, causing a food shortage and harming merchants. They sent more soldiers, some of whom were stationed in the colonists' own homes. Even more importantly, Britain took away the right of the Massachusetts colonists to elect their own leaders or hold meetings in their towns. People in the other colonies were stunned, wondering which colony would be next to suffer under Britain's restrictions.

Around the colonies, committees sprang into action. They provided money and supplies to the people of Boston. They sent messages around the colonies and promised support. For many colonists, it seemed to be time to get together and demand an end to British oppression. In Virginia, a group of leaders met and declared that Britain was denying liberty to all its colonies. They called for a meeting of **delegates** from the colonies to discuss Britain's actions.

In September 1774, 56 delegates from all the colonies except Georgia met in Philadelphia. Among them was John from New York's Committee of Fifty-One. Most of the men were strangers to one another, and they represented several different ideas and beliefs about what to do. This group, which called itself the First Continental Congress, met every day for six weeks from 11 in the morning to 4 in the afternoon.

Some delegates wanted to take a strong stand. They were willing to separate from Britain if their demands were not met. Others thought the quarrel with Britain could be patched up. John was on a committee in charge of outlining the rights of the colonies. He immediately made it clear that the colonies were protesting because they disagreed with specific restrictions imposed by Britain. While some delegates wanted an entirely new form of government, John disagreed. He was not yet ready for the colonies to break away from British rule.

John declared that it was better to correct the faults in an old government than begin a new one. He believed that the colonies could keep their form of government but drop some policies that didn't work and add some new policies that were more suited to American ideas of liberty. John and the more cautious delegates did not want to start a war. They believed they should **negotiate** with the British government. As John declared, "Negotiation, suspension of commerce, and war are the only three things. War is, by general consent, to be waived [put aside] at present. I am for negotiation and suspension of commerce."

After much discussion, the Congress drew up a document of complaints against King George III. The document said that British laws and regulations were unjust and should not be obeyed. The document was sent to all the colonies and to the king. The delegates also voted to stop trading with Britain until their rights were recognized. At the same time, the Congress asked John to write a message to the people of Britain. In it, he wrote: "We consider ourselves, and do insist that we are and ought to be, as free as our fellow subjects in Britain, and that no power on earth has a right to take our property from us without our consent. . . . Place us in the same situation as we were at the close of the last war [1763], and our former harmony will be restored."

But harmony, it seemed, could not be restored. King George III responded by sending more soldiers and warships to the colonies. The king's actions sparked open fighting in Massachusetts. When the Second Continental Congress met in Philadelphia in May 1775, the American Revolution had already begun. The city of Boston was surrounded by British warships and troops, and colonial soldiers were pouring into the area to fight. When Massachusetts asked the Congress for help, delegates voted to create an American army and asked George Washington of Virginia to be its commander in chief.

It was not easy serving in the Congress. For one thing, John lost income by being a delegate. The colonies paid their delegates very little money, around $4 a day. As he wrote, "the allowance does by no means equal the loss." John also hated being separated from Sarah, his wife of less than a year, and he missed her. When

As a delegate to the First Continental Congress, John and others met in Philadelphia at the city's state house, now called Independence Hall.

he wanted to go home for the Christmas holiday, Congress told him no. The young husband expressed his deep feelings in a letter to Sarah, writing that even if Congress did not take a break, he was going to be with her. "[D]epend upon it," he wrote, "nothing but actual imprisonment will be able to keep me from you."

While General Washington was fighting the British, the Congress still hoped that the conflict could be settled. Most of the delegates agreed with John and did not want to completely separate from Britain. John was a moderate man who was more suited to getting results with his mind and his pen. He and other delegates listened to the needs of the colonists and carefully advised courses of action.

But colonists and delegates began to change their attitudes as the fighting went on. The British government refused to recognize colonial rights and cut off all trade with the colonies. The king even sent foreign soldiers from Germany to fight the Americans. By the summer of 1776, many colonists believed that America would have to become an independent nation.

Some colonists began to support independence because of the writings of Thomas Paine. In a **pamphlet** called *Common Sense*, he called for Americans to break away from Britain and create their own nation. In the

Thomas Paine's *Common Sense* was read by thousands of colonists. General George Washington even had it read to his soldiers.

Congress, the delegates talked back and forth about what to do. Finally, after much discussion, they asked Thomas Jefferson of Virginia

Thomas Paine's *Common Sense* was one of the most influential writings of the American Revolution. It cost a penny a copy, and a total of half a million copies were sold. Because the population was so much smaller in America at that time, it would be like selling more than 33 million copies today. Thomas Paine was a good writer, and his pamphlet helped rouse the colonists to demand their independence.

to draw up a document. He wrote the Declaration of Independence, and on July 4, 1776, the delegates signed it.

John did not sign the Declaration because he was in White Plains, New York, working with the newly formed New York Provincial Congress. Part of his work included meeting with groups of colonists who disagreed about independence. Some were for independence, some were against it, and some stood in the middle. Even by 1776, as much as half the population of New York was still loyal to the king. Many of these **Loyalists** were merchants, shopkeepers, and wealthy landowners whose businesses would be hurt if the colonies broke away from Great Britain.

Although John had not originally been for

After hearing news of the Declaration of Independence, colonists in New York City celebrated by tearing down a statue of King George III.

independence from Britain, after he read the Declaration of Independence, he changed his mind and supported the **patriot** cause. He wrote a proposal approving the actions of the Continental Congress. In it he wrote that the Congress made sense when it declared independence. He wrote, "while we lament the cruel necessity which has rendered that measure [the Declaration] unavoidable, we approve the same, and will, at the risk of our lives and fortunes, join with the other colonies in supporting it."

As the war progressed, New York City became a major target of the British army. In August 1776 British soldiers invaded New York City. Although General Washington rushed to defend the city, his troops were outnumbered. After several battles around the city, Washington retreated. The British occupied New York City and held it throughout the war.

John and the New York Congress stayed outside the city and continued their work. One part of John's job involved drafting a **constitution** for New York, which was to become a state. John's efforts were important because New York was one of only five colonies to draw up its own constitution. One point that caused conflict was the use of the word "state" to define the territory of the former colony. Becoming impatient over the arguments, John wrote: "We have a government, you know, to form, and God knows what it will resemble. Our politicians, like some guests at a feast, are perplexed and undetermined which dish to prefer."

The state's constitution was finally adopted in April 1777. John believed that the document was an excellent instrument of government, and he advised other newly formed states to use it as a model. "Our constitution," he wrote, "is universally approved." John's work on the state constitution showed that he was a person who could bring together people who had different ideas and work out compromises. He was becoming a **diplomat.**

As Americans fought to gain their independence, John was asked to be the chief justice of New York State's courts. This public office made him a prominent American leader.

In Pursuit of Peace

As the war dragged on, John continued to serve New York State. He was on the Council of Safety, which regulated prisons and worked on matters of defense. He was also appointed to be head of New York's court system as the state's first chief justice. In that position, he adopted a rule that would give a full pardon to Loyalists who would sign a pledge of allegiance to New York State. In 1778, John was also appointed president of the Congress.

While John was serving as chief justice, the British formed a plan to conquer all of New York State. One British army would come down from

Canada and another would come up from New York City to meet and fight a patriot army near Albany. The plan failed, and the Americans won a great victory at Saratoga, New York, in October 1777. Not only did the victory raise the hopes of patriots, it brought help from Europe.

France, which had lost Canada to the British during the French and Indian War, had been watching the young United States. When the French government saw that the Americans could defeat a huge British army, it considered offering help in the form of supplies, ships, and military advisers. Thanks to the efforts of Benjamin Franklin, France signed a treaty with the United States in 1778 in which it recognized American independence and agreed to aid the patriots. The treaty also meant that France was again at war with Great Britain.

Americans also hoped to get money from Spain, which claimed the area of Florida and lands west of the Mississippi River. But Spain hesitated. It was not on friendly terms with Britain, but the Spanish did not trust the French either.

George Washington leads his troops in battle. Successes such as the American victory at Saratoga helped bring France into the war on the Americans' side.

And Spain flatly refused to recognize America's independence. The situation required someone who could negotiate with both nations. Knowing John's skills, the Continental Congress appointed him an **envoy** to Spain.

In 1781, John and Sarah sailed for Spain. His mission was to persuade the Spanish government to recognize America's independence and to loan money to the United States. It was also important that American ships be allowed to use the great Mississippi River to trade, but the river was under Spanish control. Although an earlier American envoy had failed to negotiate an alliance with Spain, John had high hopes for success.

John was a very experienced diplomat by this time. But his mission to Spain failed anyway. The government never actually even received him as an envoy. Spanish officials secretly intercepted his letters and read them. Letters he wrote to other officials were never answered. When he tried to discuss an alliance or money, he was given excuses. He wrote to his friend Benjamin Franklin, "This court [Spanish government officials] continues to observe the most profound silence. . . . Heretofore the minister was too sick and too busy; at present his secretary is much indisposed."

John also found himself in the middle between France and Spain. The French pressured him to report Spanish demands so that France would not be hurt by an American alliance with Spain. And the Spanish insisted on approving any negotiations between France and the United States. For the earnest and hard-working diplomat, the experience was frustrating. John began to feel that he could not trust European governments and that the United States should not rely on foreign powers. In a letter to Franklin he wrote, "In politics, I depend upon nothing but facts, and therefore never risque deceiving myself or others by a reliance on professions [offers] which may or may not be sincere."

For more than a year, John suffered as the Spanish government generally ignored him. In the end, he did get a small sum of money, but Spain never recognized American independence nor gave Americans the right to navigate the Mississippi River. Spain feared that an independent United States would expand west into Spanish territory beyond the Mississippi River. Also, Spain was ruled by a king who did not like the government of the new United States, which was founded on ideas of liberty and democracy.

For John and Sarah, it was a great relief when Franklin wrote and asked the couple to join him in Paris. The year was 1782, and Franklin was in France to begin negotiations between the United States, France, and Britain for a treaty to end the war. It now seemed possible that the United States would indeed win its independence. Even though John had failed in Spain, Franklin knew that the young man was a fine diplomat. He wrote to John: "Here [in Paris] you are greatly wanted. . . . You would be of infinite service."

John and Sarah gladly left the shores of Spain. In that unfriendly country, Sarah had often been left alone while John was working. The couple had also suffered the tragedy of the death of a baby girl. With nothing but bad memories of Spain, they looked forward to a happier time in France. There, it appeared that John would be part of a team that would draw up a treaty to end the American Revolution.

Although John still believed the French were friends of the United States, he realized that

France would want something for its help. And he was right. A French diplomat, the Count de Vergennes, proposed that the United States meet the demands of Spain not to expand its territory into Spanish lands beyond the Mississippi River. Vergennes wanted to please Spain in order to avoid any French-Spanish conflict. John also learned that Vergennes had secretly sent an envoy to Great Britain, possibly to sign a separate peace treaty.

John was alarmed. If France signed a separate treaty with Britain, all the Americans had won could be lost. Acting immediately, John sent an envoy to Great Britain to begin separate negotiations with the British government. At first Franklin objected to John's independent action. He pointed out that the United States treaty with France said that neither country would sign a separate agreement with Britain. But John persisted. Like the lawyer that he was, John believed his first duty was to his client. In this case, his client was his new nation, and his first duty was to serve the best interests of his country. John Adams of Massachusetts, who had come to Paris as part of the negotiating team, agreed with John. "[N]o wrestler," he said, "was ever so completely thrown upon his back as the Count de Vergennes."

John's diplomacy worked. After further negotiations with France and Britain, the United States signed the Treaty of Paris with Great Britain in September 1783. John had outsmarted Vergennes, who, in the end, agreed to the treaty. In addition to granting independence, Britain agreed on several American demands concerning lands in the West. For John, a major point was Britain's attitude toward America. He never lost sight of the need for his new nation to be looked upon with dignity and respect. He insisted that Great Britain stop thinking of America in terms of colonies. When he coined the term "United States," the negotiators accepted it without any argument. Strangely enough, at the time Franklin thought it was a point of little or no importance.

John (at left) stands behind John Adams and Benjamin Franklin at the signing of the Treaty of Paris. The painting is unfinished because the British representatives refused to pose.

Although John devoted much time to his work, he and Sarah still had time to enjoy their experience in Paris. By 1783, the Jay family included a son and daughter. (Eventually, John and Sarah had two sons and five daughters.) For the beautiful

The Treaty of Paris was a triumph for John. The treaty gave the United States vast new lands. When Britain agreed to give up its claim to territory in the West, the boundaries of the United States stretched at last to the great Mississippi River. Britain also gave the Americans fishing rights in the waters off the eastern coast of Canada. This was an important gain for New England fishermen. But most important, Britain recognized the United States as a "free, sovereign, and independent" nation.

and socially accomplished Sarah, Paris was an exciting place. In their home in a suburb of Paris, the couple entertained many guests.

Although John was not pleased with the actions of the French government, he made a distinction between the government and the people. Like Franklin, he greatly admired the French. In one of his letters, he wrote that while he did not especially like the French court, he had only "sentiments of good-will and regard" for the people.

The Jays received offers to stay in Paris, but they were anxious to get home to their own country. When the couple left France, John Adams praised John's work, writing: "Our

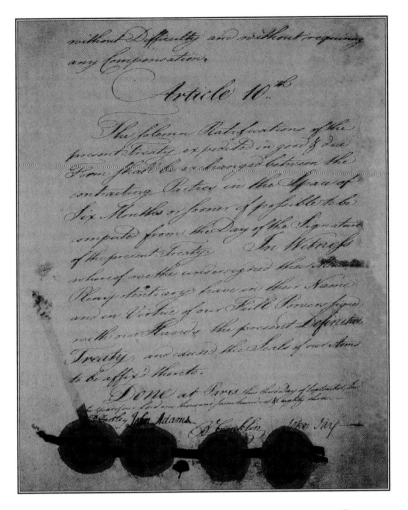

As a skilled diplomat, negotiating the Treaty of Paris in 1783 was a great triumph for John.

worthy friend, Mr. Jay, returns to his country like a bee to his hive, with both legs loaded with merit and honor."

John's beloved New York City had been occupied by the
British during the Revolution. When the city was freed, he
wanted to return to private life. But his nation called on
him once more, and he returned to public service to help
write a Constitution for the new United States.

Forming a Constitution

O nce back in New York City, John dreamed of becoming a private citizen. He built a new home for his family and wanted to spend more time there with his wife and children. At that time, New York City was the capital of the United States. Many important people came to New York City for business or to serve in the government. As they had in Paris, the Jays entertained often and were very popular.

But John was too famous to remain just a private citizen. The Congress had other plans for this distinguished diplomat. The United States still had many problems to deal with in its foreign affairs. Britain still kept several fur-trading posts in the West. Spain remained unfriendly and denied Americans the right to trade along the Mississippi River. France wanted a weak United States that would depend on France for protection.

Congress asked John to take the position of secretary for foreign affairs. While glad to serve his country, he was not happy with his first assignment. Once again he was to deal with the Spanish government, which he did not like at all. For one long and weary year, John negotiated with the Spanish envoy in New York City. Instructed by Congress, John demanded the right to trade on the Mississippi. Spain refused. It seemed that an agreement was not possible.

Then, John made a mistake. He was so worn down by the negotiations that he gave up the demand for trade on the river. In exchange, Spain agreed to sign a treaty of **commerce** with the United States. Such a treaty would benefit the merchants and traders along America's East Coast. But settlers along the western frontier would be left out. People in the West were furious. They rose in protest and even threatened to make an alliance with Britain.

Congress backed away from such a treaty, and negotiations with Spain fell apart. John also failed to persuade the British to give up their fur-trading posts in the Ohio Valley. By this time, John and other American leaders realized that the government under the Congress was just too weak and divided. They believed that unless the United States formed a powerful national government, the country would never gain the respect of other nations or be able to deal with others on an equal basis.

At this time, the United States was governed by the **Articles of Confederation,** the nation's first constitution. The Second Continental Congress had drawn up the articles, which were meant to unite the states as one nation. There was no president and no system of courts. Congress was in charge. But the articles gave a great deal of independence to the states. Congress could not raise taxes. It could only ask the states for money, and often the states refused. Congress could make certain laws, but it had no power to enforce them. States quarreled with one another over trade and their claims to land in the West, and Congress could not interfere. Under the articles, the individual states were really more powerful than the national Congress.

It seemed clear to John and other leaders like Alexander Hamilton of New York and James Madison of Virginia that the nations of Europe would not deal with such a weak government. Spain, Britain, and France were waiting for the United States to divide and fall apart. If the young country was to survive, it needed a new form of government. In 1787, Congress called for delegates to attend a convention to draw up a new constitution.

The delegates who gathered in Philadelphia that year faced a difficult task. Because of their experience under British rule, many Americans were afraid of a strong national government.

Along with John, Alexander Hamilton served as a New York delegate to the convention to draw up a constitution.

Others felt that the states should protect their rights. But the delegates knew that a strong national government was needed and that the states would have to give up some power. They would have to **compromise.**

After many arguments and compromises, in 1787 the delegates completed the Constitution of the United States, which is the foundation of our national government. Under the Constitution, the central government was divided into three branches: a **legislative branch**, with a Congress that makes the nation's laws; an **executive branch**, headed by a president to enforce the laws; and a **judicial branch**, made up of a Supreme Court and other courts with the power to explain the laws and apply them. One of the most important parts of the Constitution stated that laws passed by the government were to be obeyed above any laws passed by the states.

We know about some of the arguments and debates at the Constitutional Convention because of James Madison of Virginia. He kept a detailed journal of all the proceedings. But Madison did more than take notes. He is often called the "Father of the Constitution" because he was willing to compromise. When delegates could not agree, Madison suggested ways to solve the problem. Many of the parts of the Constitution that delegates agreed on were the result of the compromises suggested by James Madison.

But the final test was still to come. For the Constitution to become the law, 9 of the 13 states had to **ratify** it. Not all states were pleased with the document. Some states felt their rights were taken away. Others believed the government was simply too strong. Some merchants feared the government would interfere with their trade. Many small farmers thought that large land-owners and businesses would gain control of the government.

John strongly supported the Constitution. He and some other leaders knew that the Constitution was essential for the survival of the United States. These men and others who supported the Constitution were called Federalists. Those who opposed the Constitution or wanted to change it were called Anti-Federalists.

Because they were prominent leaders, people would listen to John Jay, Hamilton, and Madison. To persuade the states to approve the Constitution, these three men wrote a series of newspaper articles called *The Federalist Papers.* These articles

As one of the contributing writers of *The Federalist Papers,* John explained why he thought a strong national government was extremely important for the new nation.

are considered to be the best ever written to explain and defend the American form of government. Although John did not write that many of the papers, he wrote from the mind and heart of an experienced diplomat. He addressed much of his argument to New York State. As a large and powerful state, it was important for New York to ratify the Constitution.

Because of his experiences, John was especially concerned with what foreign nations could do to the United States if it continued to be weak and divided. Possible wars were on John's mind when he wrote that "nations in general will make war whenever they have a prospect of getting anything by it." Britain and Spain still controlled lands on American soil, and John warned that a weak United States might invite war from European powers. He also pointed out the necessity of trade and commerce for Americans. And he argued that the United States had to have a strong central government that could make lasting trade treaties with other nations.

John also wrote about the concerns of people who thought that an executive branch with a president would be too strong and might behave like the king of England. He noted that the Constitution called for a president who would only be elected for a few years. Those who elected the president, John wrote, would be "composed of the most enlightened and respectable citizens. . . . those men only who have become the most distinguished by their abilities and virtue, and in whom the people [see] just grounds for confidence."

New York State delegates argued and debated for more than a month. John had written and spoken nonstop in the hope that the delegates would approve the document. At one point he posed a question to the delegates. "Suppose," he asked, "nine States should . . . adopt it, would you not in that case be obliged either to separate from the Union, or [take back] your dissent?" John's arguments finally won over the delegates, and on July 26, 1788, they voted to ratify.

It was a moment of absolute triumph for John. And others also recognized his tremendous efforts. George Washington wrote to John: "With peculiar pleasure I now congratulate you on the success of your labors to obtain an unconditional ratification."

Once the Constitution was in effect, state

When New York State ratified the Constitution, New York City celebrated with a parade. The float here represents a "ship of state."

officials called electors had to cast their votes for a man to lead the nation. Early in 1789, they elected George Washington to be the first president of the United States. To assist him in governing, Washington had a number of talented and honorable men to choose from. When he turned to John, he asked him which government position he would like.

Dressed in his official robes, John is portrayed as the first chief justice of the United States Supreme Court. John established the principle that the Court would work for the welfare and good of all citizens.

Good Laws Make Good Citizens

The Constitution had established a system of federal courts, with the Supreme Court at the head. It was the job of the Supreme Court to uphold the Constitution and guarantee the rights of all citizens. Because John felt so strongly about the Constitution, he chose the position as chief justice of the Supreme Court. But first he had to be nominated by the president, and Congress had to approve him. With Washington's urging, John was nominated and approved in September 1789. In congratulating John, the president wrote: "In nominating you for the important station which you now fill, I not only acted in conformity with my best judgment, but I trust I did a grateful thing to the good citizens of these United States."

The Supreme Court included five other men, called associate justices. They met for the first time in New York City in February 1790. In one of his first speeches in a court case, John spelled out the principles and ideals of the Constitution and good government. "Let it be remembered that civil liberty consists not in a right to every man to do just what he pleases; but it consists in an equal right to all the citizens to have, enjoy, and do, in peace, security, and without [harm], whatever the equal and constitutional laws of the country admit to be consistent with the public good."

Although John did not oversee important court cases, he did establish important principles of government. With his guidance, it became clear that the Supreme Court would not be influenced by the executive branch or the legislative branch. The Court would be an independent body. John also made it clear that the rulings of the Supreme

Court had to be obeyed by the states.

At that time, part of John's duties included holding court sessions in the different states. Although he was often ill, he would still ride around the countryside on horseback. John was very popular and welcomed wherever he appeared. He was described by a person who saw him in Boston: "The expression of his face was exceedingly amiable. . . . His manner was very gentle and unassuming."

While John served as chief justice, U.S. relations with Great Britain had become tense. Along the frontier in the West, the British were giving guns to Native Americans, who often attacked American settlers. Many believed that the British were urging these attacks on settlers to drive them out so Britain could take over the area. At the same time, the British were seizing American merchant ships in the Atlantic Ocean and forcing American sailors into the British navy. Britain also kept American ships from trading in the islands of the West Indies, which Britain

controlled. Trade with the West Indies was important to American commerce. Apparently Great
Britain believed the United States was too weak
to respond. It seemed that war might be coming.

Well aware of John's diplomatic skills, George
Washington asked him to leave the Court for a
time and negotiate a treaty with Britain. But the
choice of John as an envoy caused controversy.
Although he was a strong Federalist, he also
admired Great Britain and its people. The Congress, which had to approve his mission, was
reluctant to let him go. John himself hesitated. He
knew that many still hated and resented Britain
and that his own popularity among Americans
could be hurt if he was not successful. As he
remarked, "No man could frame a treaty with
Great Britain without making himself unpopular."

When John arrived in London, England, in
1794, he was welcomed by British officials. They
knew how he felt about Britain. John was in a
difficult spot. He had to persuade the British to
give up their trading posts in the West. He also

John enjoyed visiting the city of London, but the treaty he made there with Britain was a disappointment to many Americans.

had to make them stop seizing American ships. And he had been instructed to get a trade treaty.

After months of negotiations, the treaty was completed. The British did give up their posts in the West. They also allowed small American ships to trade in the West Indies. But American ships could not take goods from the West Indies to other parts of British-controlled territory, such as

Canada. Worst of all, the treaty did nothing to stop Britain from seizing American ships and sailors.

When John returned with the final treaty, the Congress was totally shocked. But they finally approved "Jay's Treaty." When the public heard about it, there was a tremendous protest. Most merchants were especially angry over the trade restrictions. Other people were furious because there was nothing to stop the British from taking American ships and sailors.

John was right about what would happen to his popularity. In some places, people burned straw figures of John in the streets. Others called him a **traitor** who had sold out his country for money. When Alexander Hamilton tried to defend him in a public meeting, people pelted Hamilton with stones.

In spite of the uproar, George Washington supported the treaty. He knew the United States was too weak to fight a war. The treaty brought peace and gave the young nation a chance to get on its feet. The treaty was also important because it showed that only a few years after the American Revolution, Britain was willing to negotiate with its former colonies.

An added benefit of Jay's Treaty involved the Spanish. When Spain learned of the treaty, its government joined France in a war against Britain. Now it was to Spain's advantage to deal with the United States. In 1795, Spain finally gave in and allowed Americans to trade freely along the Mississippi River.

As time passed, Americans came to see that the treaty John had negotiated did benefit the United States. Although John never negotiated again for the United States, he did not give up public life. While he was in England, his friends had put up his name for election as governor of New York State. John accepted the offer and resigned as chief justice of the Supreme Court. He was tired of the constant travel, and he also felt that the federal courts did not have enough power and influence.

In 1795, John took the oath of office as

governor of New York State. Right at the beginning of his first term, he told New Yorkers his ideas of government. He intended, he said, to "regard all his fellow citizens with an equal eye, and to cherish and advance merit wherever found." In keeping with this principle, he worked to free the slaves in New York State.

When the United States Constitution was written, there had been heated arguments over the issue of slavery. Many delegates wanted to do away with slavery. Others wanted to keep it. In the end, the Constitution did not eliminate slavery. But after the American Revolution, states in the North began passing laws to gradually free the slaves in their states. New York was among these states.

As early as 1785, John and other leaders in New York State had founded a society to encourage the freeing of slaves. John was the society's first president. New York also passed a law banning the sale of slaves in the state. Thanks to John's efforts as governor, in 1799 the New York legislature passed a law that all children who

As governor of New York State, John began the effort to prohibit slavery in New York and free the state's slaves.

were born to slave parents after July 4 of that year would be born free.

John served two terms as governor. At the

end of his second term, in 1801, he turned down the chance to become president of the United States. He was 56 years old and had given nearly all his life to public service. It was time to retire. John and Sarah left New York City, moving to a home in Bedford, New York. Shortly after the move, his beloved Sarah died. John lived on in Bedford, keeping in contact with his children and his many friends.

John died on May 17, 1829. He was recognized as one of the most important statesman of his time. He had strongly supported the Constitution and successfully persuaded others to give their support. As a diplomat, he helped guide a young United States through difficult times. While John Jay was a moderate man who was never extreme in his views, he still took independent action when it was needed. As he himself said of his public life, he never hesitated to express his ideas about "such important public measures as, in my opinion, tended to promote or retard the welfare of our country."

GLOSSARY

Articles of Confederation–rules and regulations set up by the Second Continental Congress in 1781 to govern the United States

colony–a land or territory ruled by another country

commerce–buying and selling of goods among people, groups, and nations

compromise–an agreement that is reached when both sides in an argument give up some of their demands

constitution–a plan of government explaining what that government can and cannot do

delegate–someone who speaks and acts for others

diplomat–a person whose job is to handle relationships among groups or countries

envoy–a messenger

executive branch–the part of the U.S. government that is led by the president and carries out the laws made by Congress

frontier–a place where lands that are settled meets a wilderness

Huguenot–a member of the Protestant religion in 17th century France

judicial branch–the part of the U.S. government that explains the meaning of the Constitution and the laws passed by Congress

legislative branch–the part of the U.S. government that makes the laws

Loyalists–American colonists who remained loyal to Britain during the American Revolution

negotiate–to hold discussions to find agreement

pamphlet–a small booklet

patriots–American colonists who supported independence from Britain

persecution–the oppression of a person or group because of their ideas or beliefs

proclamation–an official statement

ratify–to approve of something, such as a document or agreement

representative government–a government in which the people have a say in how they are governed

traitor–a person who betrays his or her country

treaty–a document that outlines an agreement, usually between nations, which each approves and signs

CHRONOLOGY

1745	John Jay is born December 12 in New York City.
1759	Enters King's College in New York City.
1764	Graduates from King's College.
1768	Sets up a law practice in New York City.
1773	Appointed to a royal commission to work on border dispute between New York and New Jersey.
1774	Marries Sarah Livingston; appointed delegate from New York to the First Continental Congress; is member of convention that drafts New York State Constitution.
1777	Elected chief justice of New York State.
1778	Appointed president of the Second Continental Congress
1781	Appointed an envoy to Spain to negotiate a commercial treaty.
1782–83	Helps negotiate the Treaty of Paris, which ends the American Revolution.
1784–89	Serves the Congress as secretary for foreign affairs.
1787	Writes several Federalist papers urging states to ratify the U.S. Constitution.
1790	Begins serving as first chief justice of U.S. Supreme Court.

1794	Negotiates Jay's Treaty with Britain; resigns from Supreme Court.
1795	Begins first term as governor of New York.
1801	Retires from public life after serving two terms as New York's governor.
1829	Dies May 17 in Bedford, New York.

REVOLUTIONARY WAR TIME LINE ═══

1765 The Stamp Act is passed by the British. Violent protests against it break out in the colonies.

1766 Britain ends the Stamp Act.

1767 Britain passes a law that taxes glass, painter's lead, paper, and tea in the colonies.

1770 Five colonists are killed by British soldiers in the Boston Massacre.

1773 People are angry about the taxes on tea. They throw boxes of tea from ships in Boston Harbor into the water. It ruins the tea. The event is called the Boston Tea Party.

1774 The British pass laws to punish Boston for the Boston Tea Party. They close Boston Harbor. Leaders in the colonies meet to plan a response to these actions.

1775 The Battles of Lexington and Concord begin the American Revolution.

1776 The Declaration of Independence is signed. France and Spain give money to help the Americans fight Britain. Nathan Hale is captured by the British. He is charged with being a spy and is executed.

1777 Leaders choose a flag for America. The American troops win some important battles over the British. General Washington and his troops spend a very cold, hungry winter in Valley Forge.

1778 France sends ships to help the Americans win the war. The British are forced to leave Philadelphia.

1779 French ships head back to France. The French support the Americans in other ways.

1780 Americans discover that Benedict Arnold is a traitor. He escapes to the British. Major battles take place in North and South Carolina.

1781 The British surrender at Yorktown.

1783 A peace treaty is signed in France. British troops leave New York.

1787 The U.S. Constitution is written. Delaware becomes the first state in the Union.

1789 George Washington becomes the first president. John Adams is vice president.

FURTHER READING

Denenberg, Barry. *If You Lived at the Time of the American Revolution.* New York: Scholastic, 1998.

Jay, John, Alexander Hamilton, and James Madison. *The Federalist Papers.* New York: Viking, 1989.

Lungguth, A.J. *The Men Who Started the American Revolution.* New York: Simon and Schuster, 1989.

Meltzer, Milton, ed. *The American Revolutionaries: A History in Their Own Words 1750–1800.* New York: Harper Trophy, 1993.

Paine, Thomas. *Common Sense.* Ronald Herder, ed. New York: Dover Publications, 1997.

INDEX

PICTURE CREDITS

page

ABOUT THE AUTHOR ══════════

PHELAN POWELL wrote for her college newspaper in Boston and created a cartoon strip for the same. As a Coast Guard reservist, she worked in the public affairs office and dealt with press relations. Powell has worked as a daily correspondent for the *Michigan City News-Dispatch* and is the author of biographies on hockey star John LeClair, comedian John Candy, actor Tom Cruise, and the music group Hanson, as well as a book on unsolved crimes.

Senior Consulting Editor **ARTHUR M. SCHLESINGER, JR.** is the leading American historian of our time. He won the Pulitzer Prize for his book *The Age of Jackson* (1945), and again for *A Thousand Days* (1965). This chronicle of the Kennedy Administration also won a National Book Award. He has written many other books, including a multi-volume series, *The Age of Roosevelt.* Professor Schlesinger is the Albert Schweitzer Professor of the Humanities at the City University of New York, and has been involved in several other Chelsea House projects, including the COLONIAL LEADERS series of biographies on the most prominent figures of early American history.